I0088118

Percy Aldridge
GRAINGER

TWO TIT-BITS
FOR ROOM-MUSIC

RMTB 1-2

(1910-12)

Study Score
Partitur

PETRUCCI LIBRARY PRESS

ENSEMBLE

Mock Morris — String Sextet with Double Bass ad lib. or String Orchestra

Violin I

Violin II

Violin III

Viola

Cello I

Cello II

Double Bass (ad lib.)

Handel in the Strand — Piano Quartet

Violin

Viola

Cello

Piano

Duration: ca. 3-4 minutes each
First performance: London, 1912
Queen's Hall
Performers unknown

ISBN: 978-1-60874-271-4

This score is a slightly modified unabridged reprint of the scores
issued in 1911 and 1912 by Schott & Co., Ltd., London.
The scores have been scaled to fit the present format.

ROOM-MUSIC TIT-BITS.

Nᵒ 1. MOCK MORRIS

for string six-some (*6 single players*)
or string band
by

Percy Aldridge Grainger. | begun 19.5.1910 | ended 4.6.1910 |

No folk-music tune-stuffs at all **are** used herein. The rhythmic cast of the piece is Morris-like, but neither the build of the tunes nor the general lay-out of the form keeps to the Morris dance shape. P.A.G.

All held within the above square is meant to be used in full in programs, where possible.

★ The double-bass part is to be played in string band performances only.

★★ The tune of bars 9, 10, 11 & 12 is (unwittingly) cribbed from an early "Magnificat of Cyril Scott's. He has also used the phrase in a piano piece "Chimes" Op. 40. Nᵒ 3, (Elkin & Cᵒ Ltd.) in which it can be consulted. P.A.G.

15
20
mp
to the fore
(marc.)
Plucked
(pizz.)
Plucked
(pizz.)
25
louden very slightly
(pochiss. cresc.)
Bowed
(arco)
div.
30
33
35
short
(stacc.)
accompanyingly
(non marc.)
clingingly, feelingly, and to the fore
(legato, espress. e marc.)
mp (or mf)

40
louden (cresc.)
mp
mf
f
to the fore (marc.)
p
45
louden lots bit by bit (poco a poco cresc. molto)
Bowed (arco)
Plucked (pizz.)
heavy (pesante)
50
53
55
very richly (molto sonore)
very much to the fore (marcatiss.)
ff

60
65
Plucked (pizz.)
Bowed (arco)
Plucked (pizz.)
Bowed (arco)
70
heavy and rather short (pesante e mezzo stacc.)
heavy and rather short (pesante e mezzo stacc.)
heavy and rather short (pesante e mezzo stacc.)
clingingly and very much to the fore (legato e marcatiss.)
Plucked (pizz.)
Bowed (arco) clingingly and very much to the fore (legato e marcatiss.)
heavy and rather short (pesante e mezzo stacc.)
Plucked (pizz.)
Bowed (arco)
heavy and rather short (pesante e mezzo stacc.)
75
clingingly and very much to the fore (legato e marcatiss.)
80
75
all the time (sempre fff)

5

105
roughly
heavy (pesante)
roughly.
well to the fore (marcatiss.)
roughly
to the fore (marcatiss.)
div.
short (stacc.)
Plucked (pizz.)
110
louden (cresc.)
Bowed (arco)
115
heavy (pesante)
Plucked (pizz.)
louden (cresc.)
120
Lay down bow
don't soften (non dim.)
richly (sonore)
well to the fore (ben marc.)
heavy (pesante)
Bowed (arco)
div.

125
130
Plucked
(pizz.)
lots (molto)
well to the fore
(marc.)
Plucked
(pizz.)
Bowed
(arco)
lots (molto)
135
140
lay down bow
Plucked
(pizz.)
on with mute
(con sord.)
Muted
feelingly and clingingly (espress. e legato)
Plucked
(pizz.)
Bowed
(arco)
Plucked
(pizz.)
145
louden slightly
(poco cresc.)

150
louden
(cresc.)
div.
155
160
to the fore
(marc.)
soften
(dim.)
Mute off
(senza sord.)
to the fore
(marc.)
mp (or mf)
Plucked
(pizz.)
div.
165

ROOM-MUSIC TIT-BITS.

Nº 2. CLOG DANCE: "HANDEL IN THE STRAND."

to be played to, or without, clog dancing.

for my friend William Gair Rathbone, with thanks for the sub-title.

for three-some: fiddle, bass-fiddle (*cello*) and piano

middle-fiddle part can be left out at will.

or four some: fiddle, middle-fiddle (*viola*), bass-fiddle (*cello*) and piano.

by

Percy Aldridge Grainger. begun Feb. 1911 | ended 13.4.1912

All the parts may be doubled to any extent. For instance, it might be played on string band (without double basses) and two pianos.

In bars 1-24, 50-53, & 77-90 I have made use of matter from some variations of mine on Handel's "Harmonious-Blacksmith" tune. P. A. G.

Fiddle (Violino)

Middle-Fiddle (Viola) can be left out at will.

Bass-Fiddle (Cello)

PIANO.

FAST & MERRY. Very rigid in time. M.M. ♩ = between 120 & 132.

p shortish (*mezzo stacc*)

mp feelingly (*express.*)

5

or (*ossia*)

or
(ossia)
10
slight
(poco)
mp
(or p)
mf
(or mp)
slight
(poco)
or
(ossia)
richly
(sonore)
mf
richly
(sonore)
mf
(or f)
(thinly)
(non troppo sonore.)
p
mp
15
p (or pp)
or
(ossia)

merrily
(giocoso)
louden
(cresc.)
feelingly
(espress.)
louden
(cresc.)
louden
(cresc.)
20
louden bit by bit.
(poco a poco cresc.)
clingingly
(legato)
tellingly
(sonore)
louden lots
(molto cresc.)
don't soften
(non dim.)
soften
(dim.)
louden more
(più cresc.)
heavy
(pesante)
or
(ossia)
heavy
(pesante)
well to the fore
(ben sentito)
25
louden in the bass
(cresc.)

marked
(marc.)
marked
(marc.)
30
f
mp
f
mp
f well to the fore
(or ff) (marcatiss.)
f well to the fore
(or ff) (marcatiss.)
f well to the fore
(or ff) (marcatiss.)
mf
sf
sf
mf accompanyingly.
P * P * P * P *
35
f
(or mf)
8
f

P
40
ff fiercely
(feroce)
ff fiercely
(feroce)
ff fiercely
(feroce)
f
ff to the fore, not accompanyingly.
(prominente)
heavy
(pesante)
P
marked and heavy
(pesante e marc.)
marked and heavy
(pesante e marc.)
marked and heavy
(pesante e marc.)
45
mp louden lots
(molto cresc.)
ff

Plucked
(pizz.)
Bowed
(arco)
mp (or mf)
50
sharply and short.
(stacc. e poco marc.)
mf
(or f) clatteringly
p (or mp)
or
(ossia)
without pedal
(senza pedale)
louden
(cresc.)
louden quick
(cresc. subito)
shortish
(mezzo stacc.)
shortish
f (mezzo stacc.)
55
f clatteringly

ff to the fore
(marcatiss.)
ff to the fore
(marcatiss.)
ff to the fore
(marcatiss.)
or
(ossia)
P
P
mp
P
or
(ossia)
ff
Plucked
(pizz.)
mp
accompanyingly
(or p) (quasi accompagnamento)
Plucked
(pizz.)
accompanyingly
(quasi accompagnamento)
mp (or p)
60
tone on top (the tune should be heard well above the plucked strings.)
ff
hammeringly
fff
mf
pp
pp
mf
(pp)
P
P
P
P
P
Smoothly
65
mp
louden slightly
(poco cresc.)
mf
p
p
P

Plucked
(pizz.)
mp
(or p)
f
P
p (or pp)
accompanyingly, but feelingly
(quasi accompagnamento, ma espress.)
Bowed
(arco)
warmly
(sonore)
mf (or mp)
Bowed
(arco)
mf
(or f)
Well to the fore
(quasi solo)
70
p
pp
accompanyingly
(quasi accompagnamento.)
5
6
ppp
tonefully
(sonore)
p
delicately
(delicato)
pp
3
2
8
p
P

mp
pp
p
p (or mp)
75
pp
14
P
mp
mf
shortish
(mezzo stacc.)
80
or
(ossia)
quietly
(tranquillo)
mp
85
or
(ossia)

18

shortish
(mezzo stacc.)
clingingly
(legato)
shortish
(mezzo stacc.)
95
heavy
(pesante)
very clatteringly
Slow off lots
(molto rit.)
in time
(a tempo)
Linger slightly
(poco sost.)
take your time!
louden hugely
(molto cresc.)
not short
(non stacc.)
wait for fiddle!
(col Violino)
P__P__*
100
slide
(gliss)

top note of piano
105
(fff)
fff
Slow off.
rit.
110
f clatteringly
louden lots
molto cresc.
ffff

www.ingramcontent.com/pod-product-compliance
Lightning Source LLC
Chambersburg PA
CBHW081155040426

42445CB00015B/1898

* 9 7 8 1 6 0 8 7 4 2 7 1 4 *